THE PORTAGE POETRY SERIES

SERIES TITLES

Lake, River, Mountain
Mark B. Hamilton

Talking Diamonds
Linda Nemec Foster

Poetic People Power
Tara Bracco (ed.)

The Green Vault Heist
David Salner

There is a Corner of Someplace Else
Camden Michael Jones

Everything Waits
Jonathan Graham

We Are Reckless
Christy Prahl

Always a Body
Molly Fuller

Bowed As If Laden With Snow
Megan Wildhood

Silent Letter
Gail Hanlon

New Wilderness
Jenifer DeBellis

Fulgurite
Catherine Kyle

The Body Is Burden and Delight
Sharon White

Bone Country
Linda Nemec Foster

Not Just the Fire
R.B. Simon

Monarch
Heather Bourbeau

The Walk to Cefalù
Lynne Viti

The Found Object Imagines a Life: New and Selected Poems
Mary Catherine Harper

Naming the Ghost
Emily Hockaday

Mourning
Dokubo Melford Goodhead

Messengers of the Gods: New and Selected Poems
Kathryn Gahl

After the 8-Ball
Colleen Alles

Careful Cartography
Devon Bohm

Broken On the Wheel
Barbara Costas-Biggs

Sparks and Disperses
Cathleen Cohen

Holding My Selves Together: New and Selected Poems
Margaret Rozga

Lost and Found Departments
Heather Dubrow

Marginal Notes
Alfonso Brezmes

The Almost-Children
Cassondra Windwalker

Meditations of a Beast
Kristine Ong Muslim

TABLE WITH BURNING CANDLE

Deeply moving, this requiem, this elegy chronicling the stages of grief through multiple lyric modes, these pages are as musical as they are heartbreaking.

—ILYA KAMINSKY
author of *Deaf Republic*

As someone who has also lost a son and who has little patience for finding a "silver lining" or believing my son is in a "better place," I was deeply moved by the honesty, courage and craft of these poems, especially Paul's ability to generate fresh metaphors for the emptiness of grief. The poems face grief directly and without flinching. And they face the writer's need to give a voice and an accurate portrayal of her loved son. But most importantly, the book understands the intimate connection between grief and praise in the loss of a loved child: the inability to praise or even look up and, simultaneously, the knowledge that everything must be praised, even the pain of reading her son's journal that gives "voice after the silence." And that is precisely what *Table with Burning Candle* accomplishes; its emotionally complex rendering of suffering and love knows, finally, that "death creates a space that only love/can fill" and only love can give a voice.

—ROBERT CORDING
author of *In the Unwalled City*

Julia Paul's poem, "Like Funeral Flowers Dropping Petals onto the Floor," ends with the lines "When words are but shadow/ and stone we invent a new language." Paul's mastery of language serves her readers well. Her striking images and metaphors provide pathways to understanding the addiction illness that took her son from the world. In *Table with Burning Candle*, Paul embraces the hard task of truth-telling. She does not flinch. She wants us to know her son and his journey, as well as her own. Her poems offer us ways of coming to that understanding, in language both inventive and beautiful. This is an important book.

—PAT HALE
author of *Seeing Them with My Eyes Closed*

"How do I learn to speak the language of the dead?" "How does a mother hold onto ashes when the wind insists on taking them?" To learn how to cultivate our spiritual heurism toward the undying antagonism of grief, one must prepare a *Table with Burning Candle*. Julia Paul's intimate conversation with death over the loss of her son to heroin addiction presents as many answers as questions. The only question that remains is—are we too afraid of the answers? Are we too afraid to grieve? In a room of her own, Paul locks the door, dims the light, nestles into her chair and maternally awaits the affirmation within.

—FREDERICK DOUGLASS KNOWLES II
Poet Laureate Emeritus of Hartford, Connecticut
author of *Sinking in Moonlight Alone*

Vilomah—the Sanskrit word for "against a natural order"—is used to describe a parent who has lost a child. In *Table with Burning Candle*, poet Julia Paul journals that aberrant, out-of-kilter state. The mother of an adult son who died of an overdose, Paul offers us a seat at her table of grief, serving poems that vacillate between anguished and angry, hopeless and consumed with magical thinking. But it is Paul's rendering of a parent surrendering to their *vilomahed* state that leaves the reader with the full dimension of her devastation: "Only the after's left behind," she writes, and "They say it's best when falling / from a great height to hold / one's legs together and land / on bended knees."

—B. FULTON JENNES
author of *Blinded Birds*

TABLE
WITH
BURNING
CANDLE

POEMS

JULIA
PAUL

CORNERSTONE PRESS
UNIVERSITY OF WISCONSIN-STEVENS POINT

Cornerstone Press, Stevens Point, Wisconsin 54481
Copyright © 2024 Julia Paul
www.uwsp.edu/cornerstone

Printed in the United States of America by
Point Print and Design Studio, Stevens Point, Wisconsin

Library of Congress Control Number: 2024935372
ISBN: 978-1-960329-38-7

Cornerstone Press titles are produced in courses and internships offered by the
Department of English at the University of Wisconsin–Stevens Point.

DIRECTOR & PUBLISHER
Dr. Ross K. Tangedal

EXECUTIVE EDITORS
Jeff Snowbarger, Freesia McKee

EDITORIAL DIRECTOR
Ellie Atkinson

SENIOR EDITORS
Brett Hill, Grace Dahl

PRESS STAFF
Carolyn Czerwinski, Sophie McPherson, Eva Nielsen, Natalie Reiter, Ava Willett

To my sons, Bryan and Bradley,
for their boundless belly laughs and bear hugs
& in memory of my son, Brendan,
whose light shines on

CONTENTS

I. WHEN FLOWER PETALS FALL

II. HE SAID

III. POEM FOR MY SON

IV. DEAR DEATH

I. WHEN FLOWER PETALS FALL

My Son Kneeling in Rubble

What he couldn't say:
That he'd been swallowed whole
and couldn't see a way out. That faith
is a useless weapon against falling
sky. The weight of heaven, too great.
That he could see himself fading,
almost invisible in the mirror
of Room 214 of the Grantmoor Motor Lodge.
That he felt ancient as a gargoyle.

That his heart was crumpled tissue spotted
with blood. The pile of it in the pail,
a field of poppies. His stomach, an empty
take-out container; lungs, twitching roadkill.
That his arms were already broken wings.

That the needles had stippled his flesh.
That he was pouring out through those
tiny holes. He could imagine himself
in every puddle and every puddle was
an ocean he couldn't swim across. That
floating face up was no longer an option.

That he couldn't say something about love
without mentioning the needle. The needle
was the preacher with fiery words. That
when he begged forgiveness for his trespasses
the bulging vein forgave.

Woman with Doors for Eyes

I'm the woman whose eyes are doors
shut to the burning man who rang the bell.
His wild eyes spinning, spinning.

I'm the woman clutching a pile of ashes
while the news is burning. My house
is ablaze, my skirt's on fire.

The past tense is a vacant lot,
the future's a refusal of death,
while the present circles the fire.

With a spark of breath I birthed
bonfire. Heat from the funeral pyre
scorches my brows.

The sun is the crimson tip of a cigarette.
When it touches the horizon,
everything burns.

How does a mother hold onto ashes
when the wind insists on taking them?
How to rewrite the end of a story
that begins with a match and spoon?

From Darkness

There once was a snake
in our garbage can, thin and shiny
as a hypodermic. Its yellow eyes were sparks.

Because I remember this now,
I think of everything I have forgotten.
So many yesterdays have rushed by
like purse snatchers in a crowded mall.

I need to talk to you, my son said 362 days ago,
his voice already a river.
When what's taken away remains taken,
we ask, is love ever enough?

Grief is the taper in my window.
The candle flame devours the dark.

Candles on the birthday cake,
yellow eyes flickering like stars.
A happy memory.

Breath to flame.
Sometimes the fire blossoms,
sometimes it blinks out.

Breath, another form of wind.
Who knows where it goes when it's gone?

Summoning the River

some days I'm handed fire
carry plumes of flames
in cupped palms
until they blacken
like a saucepan
left to itself on the stove

death came for the begonias
I planted in spring
a small loss
blossoms into grief

some days I'm given a river
that turns to silver   a quiver
a mirror

on my knees
beside the river
I face myself
and my child
looks back at me

there is something about silence
the fool's gold of closure—

too easy to claim the jackpot
every time the sun spills

somedays I arrive
at the frozen
after the ashes have been scattered
I stand at the edge
where ice jams the rocks
splintering the surface
the waters below
stirring into light
a mirror instead of a map

Son as Hawk

Look up, Ma.
            I'm
        without tether
or boundary.
Ma,   I fly
        lift and rise
with the currents,
                wave
after wave.
This is my forever now,
                above history,
        above struggle
to keep blood and bone
                with body.
        My body
needed free, Ma,
                of the belt
        around my arm.
What I want
                to tell you,   Ma,
        is how awful it was
not to die.

33 Grams

Leafless trees claw at the sky,
rip it open like a wound.

Today the snow falls through.
Tonight, the stars.

The winter birds remind me of him—reaching
and falling. Sometimes, he's that distant hawk
slipping alone through the clouds.

It hurts to look up.
When I do I fall backwards.

Yesterday's worry beads wrap around my neck.
They mark me like the tattoo he talked me into
to celebrate his sobriety.

Hope was a Bob Marley song:
"Every Little Thing's Gonna Be Alright."

They say the body loses 33 grams
of weight when you die—
proof the soul has left the flesh.

Ashes are his new body.
The wind gives him wings.

When I look up, light stabs my eyes.
Still, I walk here
where feather and knife make the same shadow.

February 19th

Snow falls like clotted milk from a sour sky.
I scrape it from sidewalk and driveway,
trudge through slush for the double-bagged
newspaper tossed into the begging bushes.
The snow keeps falling and falling. The dog
refuses to go out, has to be pulled by her
leash. The plow throws snow.
Black smudge on white whirls, hawk circles.
Plow comes around again. Driver's brow
furrows, coffee sputters on the dash. Cars
snake around the corner, wipers swatting.
The hawk circles. The plow again.
A fringe of light. A glint of sun prisms
blowing snow like the beauty
of an erupting match, brief in its quivering.

Doorbell, 5 A.M.

When your child dies you pack
and unpack his things. You read what
he was reading, but avoid anything
with his signature, inscrutable
as rubble left by a house fire.
Things don't always happen
in the right order

Even when you're outside,
you remain inside. Dirt is jewelry
worn under the nails of those
with hope enough to plant seeds in spring.

You hold the harvest of love
in your arms until one day he
wriggles free. Time presses
against a doorbell. Time
is tricky math; things don't
always happen in the right order.

Things don't always happen
in the right order. Brutal as
the shape of a coffin, this Band-Aid
of passing time.

Brutal is the doorbell at 5 A.M.
Brutal is uncontrolled reentry.

They say it's best when falling
from a great height to hold
one's legs together and land
on bended knees.

Like Funeral Flowers Dropping Petals onto the Floor

We cling to our beauty.
        We refuse the autopsy
of our intentions. We live
        in dioramas made from
tissue boxes and wishbones.
        We mistake the mist
for the shape of a loved one.
        We haunt the slaughterhouse
of regret. When the wind
        blows hard, we tremble.
When we tremble
        we reach for the bottle
shaped like an urn.
        They Narcanned him
four times in the half-lit room.
        We do what we can.
At least, we do what we can.
        On the edge of our world,
we cling to our beauty.
        On the edge of the world,
we dress our wounds
        with duct tape and newspaper
advice columns.
        When words are but shadow
and stone we invent a new language.

Morning Landscape

I despise flowers, especially ones that break
winter's grasp, the daffodils and crocuses
that pop their fatuous heads out of the dark
just because the sun whistles to them
the way Raincoat Man lures children with candy.

Their eagerness to twirl skirts of pinks
and yellows in a slim fringe of light
like ballerinas in a Christmas pageant
makes me sick. Hyacinths bedazzle my yard
like faux jewels on a denim jacket. Symbols
of something they're not, these imposters of hope.

The choir sings a trash bag gospel of rebirth
and renewal even as petals begin to wilt
and drop. How hideous this spectacle
of fleeting radiance like fireworks
on a summer night. The bare bulb
that illuminates the dark corners
of my basement is more majestic
than an iris awakening to flecks of light.

Tulips struggle to unwind—stamen, pistil,
ovary, stigma. How they unfurl,
then shatter at their peak, victim
to their own urgency. It hurts to witness
the wilt and wrinkle of the bloom, stalks
bowing into loss, grief nothing more than
petals moldering in dirt, the rhythm
of leaving complete.

Overdose

Only the after's left behind. Just ask the night.
Violet bruised sky, kohl-rimmed moon,
every shade of darkness
reveals itself in layers like peeling paint.
Deletion in degrees. Destruction. Reduction. Absence.
His words turned to cinder,
silent as light on water, as chalk on sidewalk.
Every minute sighs goodbye.

Every minute sighs goodbye
silent as light on water, as chalk on sidewalk.
His words turned to cinder.
Deletion in degrees. Destruction. Reduction. Absence
reveals itself in layers like peeling paint.
Every shade of darkness—
violet bruised sky, kohl-rimmed moon.
Only the after's left behind. Just ask the night.

Discharged from All Confinement

He scrambled out of the crib at one.
Took off on two wheels at four.
Was abducted by aliens at seven.
Really I was! he insisted.

Climbed onto the roof at eleven.
Jumped from the roof at thirteen.
Walked into a bar at sixteen. Found love.

At eighteen, escaped through the gate
on the back of a spider in the shape
of a pill he mistook for a new world.

At twenty-four Broward County
discharged him from all confinement.
At thirty, made a church under the stars
and preached to the orbiting gnats.

At thirty-two, he built a cell without walls,
its bar-less windows lit by streetlight.

At thirty-three, bested Jesus. Rose from
the dead over and over, scarred flesh
jolted awake just as he was getting comfortable.

At thirty-seven, he mistook candlelight
for the moon. At thirty-seven, he stood
before the cave of wounds, a needle
instead of a lantern.

At thirty-seven, he drew chalk marks
in the shape of his body, begged the rain

to erase him. At thirty-seven, he clung
to the crumbling ledge of temporary.

At thirty-seven, he swam away in a riptide,
everyone on shore, shouting, come back!
At thirty-seven, the wind claimed the kite.
At thirty-seven, he floated free, weightless
as his name.

Prayer to Unending Sky

The damage already done
the body gone

its grit and ash
rest in the box

the artist crafted
with one of my son's canvases

he is within his own art
which would please him

to know
if knowing goes on after death

the life I gave him
has lost its spark & will

He believed not in heaven
or hell but in eternal life

        O blur of sky
with no beginning and no end
let crimson and lavender
brushstrokes emerge
within this dusk
to reveal him unbound

Self Portrait with Used Syringes

bloodstained clothes   two matchbooks

one bottlecap   a dozen

wax folds   a strap   burnt

spoons broken lighter   a plethora

of orange   caps

from discarded needles

unearthed from his   backpack   car

duffle   laid out   on kitchen table

with bowl of green apples   yesterday's

newspaper   etc

Vital Statistics

Shirt slit up the front by EMTs   (we must hold on,
the coroner removes from the body,   we must let go)
noting details:

shirt: yellow   (Smooth moons of buttons
    held by slender thread)

hair color: reddish blond,   (flax to flame)

eye color: blue,   (burning embers of azure)

height 6'2", weight 180,   (the slender thread
    is everything)

surgical scar on one wrist,   (where tiny fists
    of knots linger)

tattoo on the other,   (a mandala of desire and fate)

freckles sprinkled across face,   (the way pins scatter)

arms and legs   (fragile as hollow bones)

Time of death: (the ticking script tangling
    and untangling)

12:47 A.M   (names of things vanishing)

Dear Coroner, How Could You Know

that he was articulate, and very, very, funny,
that he once knew all the state capitals in alphabetical order,
won a prize for metalsmithing in high school,
loved reggae, Volkswagens, quesadillas with gorgonzola,
snowboarding, reading Cormac McCarthy
and that he loved how light fell through stained glass windows,
his brothers, swing sets covered in snow,
insects caught in amber, blank canvases,
the geometry of a pieced together bowl,
how sun sparked orange like matchsticks on concrete,
that he loved to dawdle like he had time in his pocket
and believed in ghosts, in not killing spiders,
and forgave, forgave the haters, the suits and shoppers
who brushed past him, muttering under their breath,
but loud enough for him to hear, *fuck off, junkie.*

Facts:

Cells of the fetus migrate across the placenta and become
part of the mother's tissue.

*

The heart is the size of a fist. It pounds and pounds and pounds.

*

Facing the day, my son once said, is like searching for a house
number in the dark.

*

Every door was buried under burned-out porchlight.
He climbed the chain link of bent spoons.

*

He did not get out of here alive but you already knew that.

*

After you die, your brain knows you're dead.
Absence takes over from presence.

*

When the kite slips away.
When flower petals fall.
When ashes scatter.

II. HE SAID

Pulled

Imagine he could return for one thing.
Would it be for the ocean?
To ride its waves without going under?

Would he still go around and around
like a trapped echo? Would he even then
be pulled into riptide by the pulsing song?

To Drown Without Water

I tell you it's possible to drown without water,
to sink below the cracked surface.

You don't need to be in the water
to find that the shore is out of reach.

You might be on a street corner
panhandling for your next fix.

The lines you spin to hook
a dollar. Withdrawal beginning

to nibble your bones. The quick
plunge of the needle into flesh.

Your eyes bobbing.
River of blood igniting.

I tell you it's possible to be
swallowed by fire without flame.

The half-lit candle in your pocket.
Tomorrow snagged on the pin of a grenade.

Mercy

This is where the line enters the water,
pierces its skin, sinks, heavy with hope.

This is where the pickerel is who can't resist
the impulse to swallow what catches the light.

Have you ever been the pickerel?
Have you ever circled the hook?

Think of the moth at the candle,
the monk ablaze in the square.

Think of the child blinded by an eclipse,
the addict chasing what can't be caught.

Mercy doesn't kill the gnat that lands on the page,
but prods it with a pencil until it flies off.

Mercy is the fisherman with beard and belly
who looks like God as he releases the fish.

This poem

holds a wound in its cup of bitter coffee.
This poem asks, *Why is the rain not black*
as the ink of its words?
This poem wants to fill a filigreed urn
with its own ashes. This poem
shoplifts from the merchant
who only has nice things to say.
This poem can swear in six languages
and talks shit about other poems,
especially ones with soul in them.
If this poem had a face, it would
never shave and its heavy-lidded eyes
would be the address on the wrong
side of the tracks. If this poem
were a saint, it would be Lawrence,
the martyr, who was grilled on a gridiron
and declared, *I'm done on this side, turn me over.*
This poem wants to talk about heaven
from the point of view of the needle.
When this poem is near its end, it will
pull off the road at the next sunset,
sit in silence until darkness erases
its scrawled lines. This poem can't explain
what it's like to be invisible but can refer
you to the absence of the puddle at the end
of the driveway or to the man nodding off
in the shadow of the alley.

Black Dot

This is what loneliness looks like,
defined by what surrounds it.
A single black balloon
slipping through white sky.

This is the period sitting
at the end of a sentence,
any sentence, including this one.

This is what God looks like
from behind closed eyes,
faceless and distant.

This is the soul
according to some.
The soul, blackened by sin,
the light of grace snuffed out.

No.

This is the needle mark.
This is the black hole
into which the self disappears.
This is the exit wound.

The Line-up

Stock-optioned pusher   pusher
in white coat   in the alley   in the aisles
of Stop & Shop   pusher
at high school parties   pusher
with free samples   with endless refills
fueling habits   fueling a Lincoln Navigator at the Citgo
pusher who does time
who gives keynote speeches   pushers
who advertise   who adulterate
who hunt you down   who shoot you
in the head   who takes insurance   pusher
with a posse   pusher
who possesses you   keeps you going
keeps you from being sick so you can function   pusher
with something to numb the pain
assassinate your soul
who writes scripts   who loads the needles
pusher with fingers on your pulse
who pushes promises   pusher
six degrees removed from you
with multiple degrees   pushers
with dirt under their nails
who sanitize their hands before touching you

pusher who looks like Jesus   Scarlett Johansson
pusher at the disturbance on the corner
of Park and Putnam   pusher
who sips mimosas at the bar   winks at you
at the red light   pusher
who tells you to fuck off when you're short or late
tells you no one else cares
pusher who sells you hell   says hello

says yo keep it on the down low
who wants to know   Blue Cross & Blue Shield?
pusher who demands only twenties   has a code
has a corner   has a company has a country
has your child

He Said

he was just tired.
Said he knew nothing
about missing change.
He was just tired.
He said what's wrong
with long sleeves?
He said he needed money
for gas, food, rent.
He needed
to be bailed out.
He said the needles
belong to Randy's brother.
Said he had to pay them back
or they'd kill him.
He said you don't understand
what it's like.
He said rehab. Said no rehab beds.
He said I have sepsis, I have Hep C.
Said I have a bed.
He said they don't know what they're doing,
I'm out of here.
He said bullshit, fuck you, I hate you.
I have a detox bed.
I just need a ride, no money.
He said I need money. He said I love you.
He said you don't understand,
I'm outside, it's pouring, it's snowing,
I'm freezing, I'll die, I have sun poisoning,
someone stole my phone,
my ID is missing, my face is abscessed,
I'm hungry, I love you. I may
have a job tomorrow, I need money today,

I have cellulitis, you don't understand,
I miss the family, I can't stop.
I need help, there are no beds,
there's a bed, I'll be honest, I used again,
I have kidney failure, you don't understand,
I just need forty, can you make it sixty, fuck you.
I haven't eaten, someone took my coat,
my prescriptions, my cell phone,
I have court tomorrow. I love you.
I need a ride, I'm on the bus,
I'm in the hospital, I'm in jail, I'm under the bridge,
I'll meet you at Save A Lot,
I was kidnapped; I owe them three hundred,
your ring's in the pawn shop, your leaf blower,
lawn mower, laptop's
in the pawn shop, I pawned my car,
tell everyone I love them, miss them,
I hate everyone. Can you bring me food,
it's the 4th of July, my birthday, Thanksgiving,
Christmas, they have a gun to my head,
can you give me twenty,
forty, eighty, two hundred,
I'm going in tomorrow, I promise,
this is it, I'll never ask again,
can you bring me dry clothes, it rained last night,
forty, sixty, a hundred, I won't ask again.
There's no bed. I need a bed.
Sixty, eighty, all you've got,
I won't ask again.
He said, this is it.
He said, I'm falling fast.
I'm falling hard.

One Summer Day

Before the needle twanged in his arm.
Before the bent spoon, bent back, the strap.
Before complaining veins.
Before a procession of scabs jeweled his flesh.
Before his half-lidded chase for what couldn't be caught.
Before sepsis. Before Hep C.
Before the trampled path into the woods behind Save A Lot.
Before unforgiving rain, endless snow, blistering heat.
Before donated blankets and gloves, shoplifted sunblock.
Before the cardboard sign held up to passing cars.
Before waiting for someone to toss their cigarette
as they entered a store so he could snatch it,
bring it to his lips and dry hump it back to life.
Before long sleeves in summer and pawn tickets
stashed under football trophies.
Before the oxy parties.
Before the root canal. The script.
The refills.
Before ashes, ashes, we all fall down.
There was a boy who loved his skateboard,
how it took him where he wanted to go,
to all that might have been.

Broken Hinges

Doors keep blowing open like bombs.
News of the son's relapse,
his name burning down the house again.

Christmas at the Citgo Station

A few drags off the cigarette.
Like an artist daubing paint on canvas,
he taps it against brick
to extinguish it, places it on the ground
to be retrieved after he uses
the bathroom at the Citgo.

A twin cam Grand Am,
Cadillac with tinted windows,
parade of SUV's gassing up at the pumps.
Passengers run into the store
and back out with coffees, cokes, chips
for kids in backseats stuffed with presents
and Shih Tzu's and grandmothers.

He exits. They brush past him
like they do the display
of shrink-wrapped logs by the door.
Flagpole thin beneath loose layers
of clothes, he bends over for the half cig,
cradles it in the palm of his hand.

He savors the moment, the way you
or I might that small gift we've ached for
and, finally, it's in our eager hands.
Our hearts lift but we can't bear
to open it because, like him, we know
how emptiness rushes in to fill the space
yearning once occupied.

Prayer in Public Bathroom

O spoon –   O strap –   O Bic –   O if –   O arm –
O vein –   O flame –   O brain – O rain –
O tarp in the woods –   O heart –   O hunger –
O handcuffs –   O dirt embedded in skin –   O release –
O shit – O if –   O neon night – O weeping moon –
O sleep –   O spoon –   O Bic –   O strap –   O bliss –
O sepsis –   O fist –   O shit – O glistening scabs –
O dust of my bones –   O sobriety –   O pee in a cup –
O droplets of days like this –   O brain of dead grass –
O terror of the shouting of my name – O vein –   O flame –
O bloodstain –   O alphabet of sorrow –   O mother –
O father –   O brother – O darkness –   O God –

Cycles

Blue Moon

Twice this month to detox.
Twice he walks away.
Twice a second chance.

Supermoon

Obsession. Compulsion.
Obsession. Compulsion.
Obsession. Compulsion.

Harvest Moon

Fastrack bus to Hartford.
The cravings consume him.
The feast at the altar waits.

Blood Moon

The needle can't find
a proper vein. A bloody mess
when he shoots up.

Wolf Moon

He paces like an animal. Tears
at scabs on his hands. Turns off
the light he can no longer bear.

Habit

Craving is beast on the prowl
                    for the promised feast.
Craving is ocean
                    turned tsunami, ruthless in its advance.
Craving is runaway train,
                    you can't jump from.
Desire is whisper. A wish.
                    A match in a windstorm.
Desire takes you by the hand
                    to detox, rehab, sober house.
Craving drags you out
                    by the heels after day four.
Desire is the call to your mother,
                    to hear her voice.
Craving is the lie you tell her
                    for money, for money.
Craving tightens the belt around your arm,
                    puts the needle into your vein.
Craving fills the space
                    between every breath.
If you breathe, you crave.
                    If you breathe, you crave.
If you breathe.

The Next Fix Liturgy

Invocation for Recovery

Lord God of the twelve steps—
Give me power to breathe,
power to dream.
Kyrie Eliescn.
My body and blood I give
to moonlight over water,
slippery path over the wet dark
of cravings.
I want to walk on water.
Vidi aquam.
I want to un-drown.
Hear my heart pounding
against the door of desire.
Ex animo.
Hear me, vessel of hex,
mottled disk of mirror,
cast off cast out
castaway. Let my cry
come unto you.
Take my arms, my scars
the war within my head.
Avé Avé I pray,
lord of second chances,
for strength
to make it another day.

* * *

Glory Be the High

Lord God of the fuck-up—
keeper of flame,
bent spoon & needle,
candle, brew & wand.

Bless this night of the living dead—
Et cum spiritu tuo
what will forever be
will be the unheard, unfelt, unspoken.
My lord master *ex nihilo,*
out of nothing comes nothing,
dust to dust—Bless me,
the dust missed by the broom.
Be with me in my prowling vigils.
Be with me in blessed oblivion,
this sacred trance. *O Deo*, sweet
diminisher of pain, obedient
to your will, in your honor
I lower chin to chest.

When His Paintings Speak

Pink says, I'm not the Buddha in the park. I'm the healing wound, the weeping child's eyes, your silent tongue. I'm darkness in disguise, the sky before flame, the faded tee shirt loved by your son. Green says, I'm not the votive in the cathedral or the bended knee. I might be an unwashed glass in the sink or that lost holiday. I'm wind pressed against grass, the sneakers your son wore when he was happy. Blue says, I'm not the tattered prayer flags or the man who strung them along the fence. I'm stained lips, the empty bowl, wasted words. I'm wings pinned under glass, a sharpened knife, the struck match. I'm the backpack left by the door. Black says, I'm not the laughing angel or the incense escaping the thurible. I'm the chair in the white room, premonition, pity and irony. I'm a series of commas snagged on the page. I'm the silence of your son's dreams.

Poem for the Homeless

Propped against a tree, in a suburb
where every driveway is blacktopped,
is a door—a shrugging, sagging,
weather-shorn door.

Beneath peeling paint, colors
surface that few would acknowledge
as beautiful for what they reveal
of spirit, purpose, struggle.

Broken hinges sing in the wind.
I have heard them on a winter day,
tree empty of leaves, the wind
lashing its whip.

There are those who cannot understand
a door, leaning on a tree, wide open
to the sky. Some would cut down
the tree to punish the door and call it justice.

They are not reminded by its presence
how we are meant to hold
each other's sorrows.

Elegy for a Charm Bracelet

Those gold charms tinkled like altar bells

when I twisted my wrist in church or class,

places silence was expected of me.

I was a girl once.

The bracelet was more beautiful than my occasions.

It was not humble.

It did not tremble when authority spoke.

Its brilliance was borrowed from the sun.

Precious, worth some money, my father reminded me
from time to time.

At night, I placed it in its velvet lined case.

One day, I did not wear it for years.

Then decades.

A mummy in its sarcophagus.

I built a life.

I thought I was a cathedral made of stone.

I thought I couldn't crumble.

When my son became a vine searching for a wall,

when my son's hunger was consuming him,

the Earth began to quiver and break open.

Everything gold was swallowed like a pill.

Litany of Eyes Before Eyes Refuse to Open

Barbed wire eyes. Eyes on Fire. Eyes the shape of mice, of carnival goldfish. Gnarled-fists-of-clouds-eyes. Eyes that speak a new language, that have seen everything. Eyes that avalanche down mountains, flood alleyways and gutters. Eyes that refuse to see straight. Eyes in the shape of coffins, spoons, flames. Eyes that reflect a city in a puddle of tears. Eyes empty and full at the same time, that roil like the ocean. Eyes in the shape of wounds, of lantern light in a cave. Bloodshot eyes, hawk-eyed eyes, glass eye, glassy eyes, black eyes, eyes like light bulbs, lying eyes, whirling angel eyes.

Last Photograph

To your distant eye, I'm a speck.
When you blink, I'll be gone
like a bug. I'm a blur

of bright yellow and blue
in this scruffy field
where green fights
its way through
an abandoned parking lot.

You could pretend I'm a flower
in a meadow and not your son
who lives under the bridge.

The giant girders of the train trestle
restrain the world above my head.
Beyond them the sky is so blue,
it's plastic.

The feral will swallow me soon
and you, you will drive away.

The Silence After Your Name

I found wax paper folds, stamped
with the image of Roadrunner in purple ink
in your jean's pockets that time
your laundry mildewed in the dryer.

You were already a shadow by then,
caught in the cross breeze of secrets and silence.

I recall the stick figure you used to draw
of yourself as a child—blue plates for eyes,
yellow spaghetti hair, watermelon-rind smile
and always, always beneath your feet, those sharp
green blades of grass that held you to Earth.

If only we could sit together again
at that diner where I bought you food
after you'd grown thin as that stick figure,

if only it were possible to talk to you
instead of to the stars at night.

In you the cycles and the storms gathered.
In you the notes of the church organ drowned.
You devoured everything, like consequence.

On your last birthday, I burned messages
I wrote to you. Smoke rose from the fire in tongues.
Turned to spark, my words were lanterns in the dark.

Praise Poem

Praise for the journal,
its opening entry that says, *I am friends
with wet boots and dirty socks.*
Praise for the artifact
of his handwriting. The beauty
of his graffiti scrawl on its cover.
Praise for the journal for giving voice
after the silence. Praise for this journal
that tells me he believed in angels.
That he saw one, wings spread wide,
at the end of a long dark street.
Praise for angels and praise for solace
and praise for the woman with sad eyes
who gave him three dollars.
Praise for his dreams and the stars
that lit them like tiny votives.
For the dream about his friend
dragging a couch across broken
asphalt onto the double yellow lines,
where he sat waiting for his mother
to come through the smog of exhaust.
Praise for his friend who shared
the couch in the woods.
Praise for woods and bridges
and all-night laundromats
where clean socks are left in a basket
by the door. Praise for clean socks
and unlocked doors.
Praise for this journal that unlocks
secrets. For sloppy handwriting
and sloppy truths. Praise
for details and literary tricks.

For saying I won't go into details
and then going into details
about licking blood from his arm
and doing pushups on bathroom floors
just to get the vein.
Praise for the courage to write.
Praise for the pen and the spiral
notebook. For its seventy-four blank pages,
each one an agony of silence.
Praise for all that is unsaid, how it echoes.
Praise the unsteady hand, the clenched fist.
Praise the pale blue lines that stretch
across these pages like a tightrope.

A Sense of Sorrow

More than the aureate ribbon of river telling time to the rimrock.
More than the hawk eavesdropping on the newly dead.

More than the thief making off with jeweled scabs of old wounds.
More than the toile curtain of night riddled with black holes.

More than the curved spine of the woman at prayer.
More than the honeyed light drawing an outline around her.

More than tendrils of thread where the button used to be.
More than a backpack hooked on the back of a chair.

More than how fast clouds can change; heaps of kisses, vessels of terror.
More than how the proof of loss is the lightning strike of memory.

More than desire's affection for high-heels and whitening gum.
More than the distant whistle, siren, bell. More than the brevity of breath.

Small Narratives

The friend you Narcanned
back to life twice
says, *as untimely as your death was,*
your life was perfectly timed.

I have nothing but the wealth
of your history now.

Someone else remembers
the chain-link vest you made
in Metalsmithing class and your
teenage fascination with Volkswagens.

Your life is broken into small narratives.

My son, I've fed you to the fire.

Your paintings live inside me.
I stole that line to give it new life.

Is the bird in the deep January
tangle of branches fact or memory?

How many times did they press on your chest?

A neighbor recalls the cookies
you baked for her that rainy day
she gave you and Ryan a ride home.

In the pocket of your jeans I find
crumpled papers with phone numbers
and empty wax folds stamped with blue ink.

Another story: diving into the reservoir,
the sky darkening, you and your
buddies running for your lives,
lightning bolts at your heels.

The last day you woke up was a Friday.
You didn't know that, did you?

Is the blinking neon light a detail I made up?

Can you hear me?
I said Nina has asked for your ashes.

I'll wash your clothes, fold them and bag them.

Tell me, where do I put the pieces
of these surfaced memories? How do I learn
to speak the language of the dead?

III. POEM FOR MY SON

Midnight Dirge

Grief sits at the table with burning candle

    & waiting cup while the kettle on the stove

        whistles like a train knifing through the night.

Autopsy Report

Dear Coroner,

When you held his heart
in your hands,
could you feel his love?
Did the world my son
breathed in for 37 years
open up to you
as you cut into his lungs?

You noted that his brain
is normal size and weight
before placing it
in the metal tray.
Did you wonder
about the memories
locked in its nest of cells?
There were many good times,
I assure you.
Once we biked
the Island of Inishmore,
explored the ancient ruins
of the Seven Churches.

His blood spilled the story
of addiction, I'm sure,
while halved organs
and tissue samples
wrote its postscript.

I don't have to tell you
how drugs rewire
the brain's reward center.
You saw the amygdala

and hippocampus
but you couldn't see
into his mind, no matter
how you probed its network
of muscles and veins.
He would've held you
spellbound
with his imagination,
creativity, dreams.

You studied his anatomy,
the atlas of his tattoos, his cage
of bones, his vessel of blood.
You calculated, analyzed,
classified, dissembled,
reassembled, recorded,
computed, reduced him
to a statistic: another overdose.

This brings me to
the question of the soul—
his soul, which gave up
the weight of being.
Tell me, did it happen
with a flicker,
the way fireflies escape
one's eye in the dark
curtain of night; or,
like a feather,
did his soul lift beyond
its terrors?
Did the ancestors gather
in song—his soul
become music?
Did you find yourself
humming as you cut?

Update

Fuck the Muzak of your Hallmark greetings.
When you slip on the dance floor,
I cheer. I hate your emoji lips,
the exclamation point of your voice.
Your laughter burns like lava. Fuck
your circus, your parades, your helium
balloons of good intentions. I reject
the engraved invitations to bake
my sorrow into a casserole for the freezer
for later or never. I reject the glitter
of your calm. Do not touch me
with your light. Do not gift me
your symbols and cycles,
shapes bent into hope. I curse
your halcyon nights, memory foam pillows.
Did I mention that your voice is a boot
to my gut? For God's sake, stop singing.
Every window sees the weather
in my face. I've draped the mirror
with tarnished prayers. Spare me
the door held open to the clearing.
I've coins in my pocket I'll never spend.

Love Letter

I stall here as an act of holding on, the way
you might linger at an open grave. Love is the tether
after death. I tell you, this page is love. When I write,

graffiti or *spoon* or *Q-tip*, I'm filling the dead space.
I write *trestle, trinity, tremble*
with love. Every comma is love. I vowel love,

pronoun love. If there were a letter in the shape
of love I'd spell every word with it.
I understand, dear reader, if you turn the page

in hope of finding whatever it is that stops
time for you. You go on, I'll stay
here a while longer in this meadow of clinging

mist, where absence takes over
for presence. Time has tossed a ball in the air.
It returns from nowhere, a memory,

and lands in the palm of my son's outstretched hand
with a sound like distant thunder.
A Band-Aid ripped off a wound

too soon excites the blood. Every mother knows that.
Wisdom insists time is the healer.
Gravity holds us in the mown grass, outside the grave.

Death creates a space that only love
can fill. *Words have wings*, a poet once said.
What else can I do but urge these words to fly?

A Winter Morning

After "Grief" by Stephen Dobyns

Trying to remember him
is like snowfall on a winter morning.
To touch the snowflake is to destroy it,
yet I can't resist opening my palm
to hold one for its brief lifetime.
Only does restless snow survive
with permission of the frozen earth
and its radiance linger with the sun's.

His name's a snowflake on my tongue.
He was mine to name.
I taught him how to print his name,
which way to face the letter "B,"
long before I called his name
into alleys and vacant buildings.

I was at the door when I learned
of his death, the frozen light
ready to break into flame.

Kintsugi

                        Thread of life
          broken
                              fragments
      of shattered glass
                      fissures
          of darkness

Take that which is broken or cracked,
      mend it with gold. The thread
            of gold joining the fragments is prayer.

Gratitude for prolonged life. Desire for strength.
      Respect for the shattered,
            for what came before the shattering.

They say an object is transformed
      by its repair, made more beautiful,
            even stronger.

                        But has it merely endured?
What of its purpose?

I broke to pieces when he died,
      like a piece of wedding china
            on a tile floor.

It's untrue that time heals all wounds.
            Every amputee knows that. Time makes you older.
            Time is the life he won't live.

This glass of wine is not gold.
      I drink it anyway to fill
            the fissures.

Yet, see, how a single streak of gold
 in the broken night
  joins sky to lake.

Survival

The lake is nervous this morning, even though
no one's drowned since 2015. With plans
for Saturday night, they were teens on thin ice.

You're skating on thin ice, mother used to say.
From a TV show I learned the best way to navigate thin ice
is flat on your belly.

Life's a gathering of survival tools, is it not?
You never know when the carabiner
might fail or the bear will startle in the path.

My father lived past 100 because he knew
how to survive everything but time.

These squirrels are preparing for winter,
tossing acorns from treetops. You could
be fooled into thinking it's raining.

Someone's always prepared for the weather,
an umbrella in the trunk, poncho in the pocket.
Another takes her chances.

Someone is digging for worms.
Someone writes a note. Another pays attention
to distant thunder, someone else comforts a friend.

This too shall pass, she says, echoing
her own mother. Leaves released
by the breeze pirouette into the lake.

Someone thinks of a soul going out, the last breath,
a screen door blowing open.
Someone else learns to float.

Saved Messages

Because we choose our form of holding on
I save these voicemail messages.

> The sound of his voice in these messages
> disrupts the dark silence of memories.

Love is the tether after death to memories
as they become shadows that waver and drift.

> In grief, time ruptures, wavers, and drifts,
> travels a river that ends in its own mouth.

Keeping it real, ma, this, from his own mouth.
In the incomplete air, the night shapes sound,

> as a river rushing over rocks shapes sound.
> My son's voice is a leafless tree in winter,

the interruption of swing sets in winter.
I want to untangle the bone-cold broken beads

> of loss, give them to the rain as it beads
> the river that, like breath, ends at the end of itself.

The way echo cleaves to the end of itself,
we choose our own form of holding on.

Elegy

He's lake and sky.
How today they become one: clouds
and their doppelgangers
on mirrored surface.
He's as impossible to hold
as water in the palm of my hand,
as untouchable
as the stars. He's every
form of light: shaft that sneaks
through the window blinds,
circle of light in a lamp-lit room,
starlight, match-flare, every spark,
glimmer, glint and glow
at the brink of day.
He's the unknowable
and the hole I dug
this morning in the garden,
into which I placed tangled
roots of rosemary.
The ripping sound
the roots made when I nudged
my thumbs into them
and pulled is also him,
as is this twinge in the knee
of my rising. The bee's
curiosity was his.
I'm helpless not to find him
in the shape every shadow makes
and in the dust
stirred by hooves and wings.

Mothering the Empty

I mother vacant landscapes,
the room, the door to which remains closed.
        I mother the silence,
the un-ringing phone,
the undying child.
        When a blanket unfolds,
I smooth out its wrinkles.
The ground is flat as relief.
        I invite myself to the picnic.
A feast of sleep. Dreams.
Where the moon fell,
        there's a hole in the sky.
The stars are heavy with grief.
After the heavens drain,
        the night becomes notebook
of inked out days.
Shadow cursives into the shape of a keyhole.

Recovery

Occasionally, we stretch the wound
to fit the fist. Sinew and tissue
keeps anything larger than a light bulb from getting in.

Inside out, we're a mess.
Bones & blood & organs; a vulture's prize.

Occasionally, we live like water that won't go
down the drain. The bathtub convinces us
we're both lake & swimmer.

Occasionally, the newspaper dances in the street
in the arms of the wind. This is both charming
and sad, like anything that is briefly now.

In one version of ourselves, we scavenge
for coins in the dark. In another, we're unharmed
even as we enter the open wound of the earth.

Solace

Branches brought down by gathering snow.
Shushed by snow, these severed limbs.

> The sigh of sky.
> The world has gone
> to its knees, as if in prayer.

For as far as I can see, no news is being made.
Out there, no one is being murdered.

> No one's overdosing,
> protesting, screaming,
> shooting, fleeing.

Cracked sidewalks, unraked leaves;
all imperfections have vanished.

> The snow has silenced,
> has softened, has glistened
> the map, has written over decay,

has censored darkness. It could be noon or it could be four.
The sundial in the garden is buried up to its face.

> Time is static. There was a time
> when static was called snow
> and televisions had rabbit ears.

The news was at six and eleven then;
not 'round the clock. This time, let the snow fall.

> Let it speak without language.
> Let the world hold
> its breath and listen.

Testament

Being of sound mind and memory.
Being of sobriety and campfire.
Being of breath and flesh.
Being of memory. And urgency.
And chipped dishes.
Being of sound. Made of sound.
My mother's voice, my mother-voice.
A plea. A pretty please.
Of sound of clouds over water.
Of sound of forgetting.
Of forgetting a face.
Being human. Human being.
Being at an impasse. Without a ticket.
Being language and lesson on a blackboard
written in chalk. Memory
of chalk on sidewalk. Hopscotch.
Throwing rocks.
Memory of motion: ballet of fireflies,
staggering home in the frozen.
I meant to say ocean. The never-
ending waves being a miracle,
not to be confused with holiness
or being whole.
I make no provision for death.
I make no provision for the nuns
who handed me hell. For the son
who has entered the seasons.
I revoke. I confirm. I swear.
I give. I devise. I, I, I am
a thin thread and not.
This is my will and my won't.

Lighting Votives in the Cathedral

You're searching still
for your son in the storm
of dust that's risen as though
someone's shaking a rug into the wind.

The black-robed priest guides
your hand, instead, toward
the faceless, haloed god
who rises from the chalice
in a gaudy galaxy of stars.

The priest is chanting, *hoc corpus,*
this is the body, *hic est sanguis,*
this is the blood, as if he knows
how to bring back the dead.
Take this cup, he insists.
The wafers that spill into your mouth
are dry as ash.

March

The sky hurts
brilliant blue
the sorry god
delivers crocus
to the hidden
map of gardens
and sunlight
to chrome
the curve
of cloud

broken into thaw
the ground
releases children
their god
clumsy
as a drunk
spills feathers
and calls it rain

changeling god
turns hands
into fists
that wheel
in the air
and birds into
prayer while
language curls
into sobs

offering ash
in place of
blood and bone
the quiet god
shrugs and
walks away

Suppose

Suppose the porch chimes possess
language and the cursing never stops.

Suppose grief becomes landscape
where the sun rises every morning.

Suppose clouds are mirrors
that reflect our terrors

and rain becomes nothing
but lists of reasons to live.

Suppose our words don't have weight
and our hands and feet are not full of nails.

Suppose the two-sides of sky
were flipped like a mattress

and God came tumbling down.
Suppose God comes tumbling down

and lands on a poultry farm
surrounded by breast-bloated chickens

adrift among the glitter of feed.
Suppose God, at that moment, understands

our discontent. Suppose instead
of metaphor the afterlife is here.

Suppose the soul's purpose
is to absorb fate like a paper towel.

Suppose it folds itself into origami,
and bird-like, escapes our flesh

in the nick of time, every time.
Suppose we are meant to fly.

This Aspect of Life

1. Each pair of eyes, a story. Hers speak another
   language. His saw a car crash into a liquor store.
   Mine drowned in the Atlantic. Yours look like
   baby mice. Lid-watching of the dying is a lost
   medical art. Hippocrates was a proponent.

2. Hidden among branches, prayer ties break into blossom.
   Even the heart isn't shaped like a heart. The heart's
   fist knocks on my door. *There's no escaping*
   the weather, my mother always said. Shadows roll over
   mountains. Rain is not to be confused with miracles.

3. I once knew a man who had "paradise" tattooed
   on his chest. What is the point of a point of view
   without the benefit of fantasy? Tonight the stars
   are a thousand-piece puzzle. Wind shifts the darkness.
   My silent hawk opens his wings.

4. The blink of porchlight. Petals abandoning
   their own beauty. Circles on a map. Map on a lap.
   A cup of sugar, two of flour, greased pan.
   Dragonfly resting on an oar, against vanishing.
   Barbed wire, broken sandals. The work of grief.

5. These are the holy moments between _____
   and _____. It doesn't take much to love
   a _____. If only _____,
   then it wouldn't _____. The eyes have it.
   Regarding loss, there are feathers still to be gathered.

Flesh and Bone Doxology

Bless my son's body,
his eyes that once held the sky,
fingers that buttoned and unbuttoned
the daily rituals.
Bless the miracle of first flutterings
the butterfly un-cocooning,
the wingspan of him as a man.
Bless the arms brailled with sorrow,
the darkness that the needle couldn't reach.
Bless the man-body in its release,
the length of him filling the gurney
wheeled from a room.
Bless the exquisite pain of birth,
and all the firsts. Remember the firsts—
the stuttered steps, sounding of vowels.
Bless all the moments from this moment on.
And all the lasts:
straightening the thin blanket,
hand pressed to shoulder,
the kiss.

Entreaty in the Small Hours

Meet me where seashells
are tombstones for lost souls,
where unanswered prayers go.
We will not be lonely there.

Meet me in August in the vineyard
of numbers where nine lives,
second chances, and things that happen
in threes co-exist. Dust and ash
will put out the welcome mat for us.

Meet me in a web of silk,
intricate and small as a spider's,
how it withstands hurricane winds
yet sparkles in rain
like a jewelry store window.

Meet me at the end of oxygen,
where drift is and exist isn't,
or is. We'll find each other in wilderness
without a compass, where stars
will shout our names.

Instead

Instead, let this bowl
hold my grief,
the way it does
newly bought
avocados,
hard as bullets,
until their flesh
gives way to touch.

Instead, let the plank
of light the sun
tosses through
this window become
door or ladder.

Let the rain
wash away
the graffiti
on the walls
of my heart.

Instead, the obituary
will be an acre
of swept leaves,
the hard work done,
tools returned
to the shed.

Tomorrow will
be field,
clinging mist,
a crown of clouds,
a silver platter
of polished sky.

Instead of storm,
I will say: child
spirit
feather

On Buying a Paddleboard after
the Death of my Son

The salesman who said February's the best time to buy a paddleboard
had a nice smile and was around my son's age.

I wanted to hug him for his mother who was probably not,
at that moment, thinking how lovely he is.

I had paddleboarded once on Cochiti Lake.
It was like floating on sunlight.

There were no sharp edges.
The lake was boundless.

The lake was gentle.
It was the life I longed for.

It was the life I longed for
for my son.

I want to focus on the distance while slipping past it.
I want my balance back.

I want to lift my eyes to the sky
without going under.

I want to float while on bended knees.
I want to stand on my own two feet.

If only the wind would take me away.
When I unclench my fist, the wind will take him away.

When I fall, the water will release me over and over.
I want to be brave enough to float again.

Poem for My Son

This is the poem in which you don't die.
This is our hour to be together. The doorbell doesn't ring yet.

Yesterday, I rearranged furniture—
a table in front of the south-facing window.

In place of Peace Lilies, begonias
and geraniums, their stems reaching toward the light.

In this poem, we've just made tacos
or spaghetti. You're laughing at your own jokes,

telling your brothers about times you snuck
out of the house, how you always got away with things.

In this poem, I say, *I love you. Be safe.*

There are so many details to see to. To bring you back
is to give you shape and smell, cell by cell.

There's birdsong outside this window. The bush by the door,
the one I never learned the name of, is budding.

The Earth is coming to Spring.
In this poem, the whole world wants to wear your face.

A Night of Now

I'm not dead, my dead
son said. I've just been
away for a few months
with the one I love.

We thought you were
dead! I said to my son
as I ran my hands over
his face like the blind
do when they want
to know. It was not
cold and stiff.

We had your funeral.
Did you go?
Yes, and it was lovely,
really touching, he
said as he was
leaving again but
not out the door.

This time he knew
where he was going.
That familiar stride.
His stride. I could
recognize it from
a mile away. Like
he was walking
on air. *Mr. Cocky*,
I said, instead
of goodbye.

4 A.M.

Apologies to the moon I cleave with my knife-eyes.
I'm sorry, echo, for the mantra of sorrow.

There might be music in the old radiator.
I regret my indifference, night.

Abundance. Too much. Silence. The emptiness
of 4 A.M. What passes for a life slips through

the minutes like hall light under a closed door.
I make promises to remember the dead.

In daylight, the dead resemble breath.
That time has no shape is not the issue here.

When I was a child, clocks went around
like a merry-go-round. The seconds were invisible.

The ordinary was written in chalk.
When I was a child there was magic

in shadows. When I was a child
there were chandeliers everywhere.

Now, I'm a Rubik's Cube of unwritten syllables,
the raspy-voiced hello to the gentle blink of porchlight.

The work of grief is river winding itself around
boulders. The work of grief is making room for absence.

Give it a room of its own without the ill-fitting boots
squatting in the corner. Give it a burning candle on a table.

This room is not where I break and enter. The dark
is soft as fleece. It smells like rain, like music.

There's a Lithuanian word that means
to name something is to make it disappear.

Imagine, a single word holds all that. I'm thinking
about something for which there's no word.

What do you call it when it's not a wolf?
On the edge of darkness, I see only eyes.

On the edge of darkness, I hear trees branching,
a hinge rusting. Something winged flies past.

IV. DEAR DEATH

Dear Death

Is it true what they say—that there's an existential slap the moment we realize you've come for us? Although, you do fuck up. From time to time, someone escapes your grasp and tells of white light and a tunnel. Meh. Trickster, you are not a travel guide. We live in your shadow, the Bible says, but you saunter in and out of our rooms like a nosy house guest. I saw you in my mother's eyes, my brothers' eyes, until you pulled the drapes and blocked the light. Fate, we may call you, but you've gone by many aliases —Morai, Morta, Atropos, you who snip the thread when time, when luck, runs out. Your sister, Clotho—such a know-it-all, stands beside the cradle doing her calculations like a NASA scientist. How rude to set the countdown clock before we've opened our eyes to this world.

O Death, that single cancer cell awaits your signal. Toy on the staircase awaits your signal. The needle waits again and again. It loves to beat you at Russian roulette. A deft hand, you have. And you come in all disguises. Old age is what most of us prefer, although, sometimes, you drag that out too long. I do try to be philosophical about you. After all, I don't know what it is to be dead. Maybe it's wonderful, fabulous, a huge improvement. Foolish, perhaps, we are to fear you.

After you took my son, some said, *he's in a better place now.* You know, the human spirit and all that; we're either full of hope or full of shit. No one said to me, death is the abyss. Nothingness. But we just don't know, do we? Because we don't know, we try to avoid you. That's what life is —undeath. You stalked my son. Dangled above his dreams. You kissed his lips more than once when he'd overdose and before the Narcan startled him back. You've got him now. Your job is done. Dear Death, you loved him too well.

I am still trying to sort things out, Death—what you've taken and what you left behind. His smell is gone, his laugh, his beautiful, sad eyes—all what one expects of you. I have his ashes. I've run my fingers through them, the way I used to run my hands over my swollen belly to know him before he was touchable. And I have memories. O Death, you've heard every cliché, I'm sure. *May you find comfort in the memories*. Maybe. Maybe someday. Today, every memory is a knife, my mother-heart your target practice. You would not take me in his place. Will not return him to me. No ransom tempts you. I don't speak your language. There's no translation for grief. It comes in the shape of a scream, in the shape-shift of clouds, in the shape of a blade left in the wound.

With teardrops of flame.

From the bottom of my frozen dark.

Because I breathe broken.

I am. Will be. Always.

Until then,

When Not to Speak

With wings that hold a galaxy,
a dragonfly kneels
before its own reflection.
A leaf in the shape of hope
vanishes when I enter.
From the silence of the lake
I learn the language of grief.
Above, the sun haloes gold
for someone praying for light.
My body's the shape of inky darkness.
Weight and weightless. I am
this cadence, here, where I can't breathe.
Everything I want to say
comes out stone-whetted, weedy.
Here is an unwritten letter,
the stationery still in the box.
Here, beseeching tongues
writhe. Here, below the mirror,
wavy and winging, a hook.
Or is it an eyelash? Hush,
says the corpse, let me explain.

ACKNOWLEDGMENTS

My deep gratitude goes out to Dr. Ross K. Tangedal, Director & Publisher of Cornerstone Press, for selecting my manuscript for publication. Thank you to Grace Dahl for living up to her name by acting with utmost grace throughout the editing process. Thank you as well to media director Ava Willett, sales director Natalie Reiter, and sales manager Sophie McPherson for being on my team. This book comes from the greatest loss a parent can suffer. I am deeply appreciative of the care and respect it received from Cornerstone Press.

Thank you to my *Partners in Poetry*—Christine, Debbie, Elaine, Ginny, Joan, Nancy, Pat, and Sherri, and to the *Murphy Morphs*—Emily, Linda, Maria, and Rina. These poems were elevated by your encouragement as well as your collective critiques. I treasure your friendship, talent, and support.

To Elizabeth, Liz, and Miriam—the struggle is real, and because of you I never felt alone. Blessings and more blessings to you.

I do not know where I would be today without the family that has lifted me up with their boundless love: My parents, Julia (1921–2017) and Edward (1918–2019); brothers Ed, Peter, Ken (1945–2002), John, Chris (1957–2014), Bob (1959–2016), Mick, and of course, my one and only sister among seven brothers, Loretta.

As always, thank you to my sons, Bryan and Bradley, for the great gift of joy. I love you more! There will always be food in my fridge for you!

* * *

Gratefully acknowledged are the following publications, where poems first appeared in earlier versions:

"33 Grams", "Flesh and Bone Doxology", "My Son Kneels in Rubble" (under the title "The Penitent Kneels in Rubble"), "Self Portrait with Used Syringes": *Mud Season Review*

"Christmas at the Citgo Station": *Hartford Courant*

"Cycles": *Sandy River Review*

"Dear Coroner, How Could You Know": *The Pushcart Prize Best of the Small Presses* (2023)

"One Summer Day", "Praise Poem", "Small Narratives": *Here: a poetry journal*

"Black Dot", "He Said", "This Poem" were published in the chapbook *Staring Down the Tracks* (The Poetry Box, 2020).

"Black Dot" was nominated for a Pushcart Prize (2020).

"Kintsugi", "Splintered Time": *Brown Bag*

"Mercy", "Suppose", "Survival", "When His Paintings Speak": *The Awakenings Review*

"On Buying a Paddleboard after the Death of My Son": *Radar Poetry*

"Poem for My Son": *Mom Egg Review*

"Poem for the Homeless" (Overneath Books, 2022)

"Son as Hawk": *Entropy*

"This Aspect of Life": *Gleam: Journal of the Cadralor*

Julia Paul is the author of *Staring Down the Tracks* (2020) and *Shook* (2015). In addition to publication in numerous literary journals, both national and international, including *Comstock Review, Minerva Rising, New Mexico Review, The Fourth River, Windmill* and *Connecticut Review*, and anthologies such as *From Under the Bridges of America, The Heart of All that Is*, and *Lavandaria*, several of her poems have been performed in stage productions. Paul served as the first Poet Laureate of Manchester, Connecticut (2014–2019), and she currently serves as president of the Riverwood Poetry Series, a longstanding reading series in Hartford, Connecticut.